Strategic Studies Institute
and
U.S. Army War College Press

THE EFFECTIVE USE OF RESERVE PERSONNEL IN THE U.S. MILITARY: LESSONS FROM THE UNITED KINGDOM RESERVE MODEL

Shima D. Keene

January 2015

The views expressed in this report are those of the author and do not necessarily reflect the official policy or position of the Department of the Army, the Department of Defense, or the U.S. Government. Authors of Strategic Studies Institute (SSI) and U.S. Army War College (USAWC) Press publications enjoy full academic freedom, provided they do not disclose classified information, jeopardize operations security, or misrepresent official U.S. policy. Such academic freedom empowers them to offer new and sometimes controversial perspectives in the interest of furthering debate on key issues. This report is cleared for public release; distribution is unlimited.

*****

*****

Comments pertaining to this report are invited and should be forwarded to: Director, Strategic Studies Institute and U.S. Army War College Press, U.S. Army War College, 47 Ashburn Drive, Carlisle, PA 17013-5010.

*****

This manuscript was funded by the U.S. Army War College External Research Associates Program. Information on this program is available on our website, *www.StrategicStudies Institute.army.mil*, at the Opportunities tab.

*****

*****

The Strategic Studies Institute and U.S. Army War College Press publishes a monthly email newsletter to update the national security community on the research of our analysts, recent and forthcoming publications, and upcoming conferences sponsored by the Institute. Each newsletter also provides a strategic commentary by one of our research analysts. If you are interested in receiving this newsletter, please subscribe on the SSI website at *www.StrategicStudiesInstitute.army.mil/newsletter*.

FOREWORD

The U.S. Army and the British Army are undergoing similar processes of rebalancing between regular and reserve personnel. The British armed forces are currently at a more advanced stage of this change than the United States, and consequently there are useful lessons to be drawn from their experience to date. This is particularly the case in a time of growing defense austerity; in addition to their smaller scale, the United Kingdom's (UK) armed forces have great familiarity with undertaking missions and maintaining close to full-spectrum capability while subject to severe and apparently insurmountable resource constraints. Studying how this is made possible may also provide valuable pointers for a U.S. defense force in an era of sequestration and budget cuts.

This monograph presents research by Dr. Shima Keene, a defense analyst with extensive experience of working both with and within the UK's Reserve Forces. Dr. Keene identifies areas where the U.S. Army and other services can potentially benefit from examining the UK's comparable program of reserve reform. Equally important, she identifies key areas where aspects of this reform have been entirely counterproductive, and points to specific and expensive recent British mistakes which it is essential for the U.S. military to avoid.

The Strategic Studies Institute considers that this monograph provides a useful view of prior experience in organizing and integrating reserve forces, and is a valuable addition to the debate on how to plan the future shape of the U.S. Army.

DOUGLAS C. LOVELACE, JR.
Director
Strategic Studies Institute and
    U.S. Army War College Press

ABOUT THE AUTHOR

SHIMA D. KEENE is a Director of the Conflict Studies Research Centre, Oxford, the United Kingdom (UK), as well as Director of the Security Economics Programme at the Institute for Statecraft, London. She is also a Deployable Civilian Expert (DCE)[1] and a member of the UK Civilian Stabilisation Group (CSG)[2] specializing in Intelligence and Security Sector Reform. She is a former Senior Research Fellow and Advisor at the Advanced Research and Assessment Group, Defence Academy of the UK, and Special Advisor to the UK Ministry of Defence (MoD), where she had responsibility for assessment and recommendations for the development of financial counterinsurgency strategies in Afghanistan. Dr. Keene advises and works closely with a number of British and international organizations on a number of topics relating to national and international security including the MoD, various UK government departments and law enforcement agencies, the Organization for Security and Co-operation in Europe, the Council of Europe, Global Futures Forum, the North Atlantic Treaty Organization (NATO), U.S. Government departments and law enforcement agencies, and various global private sector organizations. Dr. Shima has 25 years of practitioner experience in a number of industries to include finance, defense, security, and telecommunications in both the public and private sectors, with government departments, law enforcement, telecommunications, and finance. She is also a former British Army reservist soldier with 7 years military service, most of which was spent serving as the Company Medic and Physical Training Instructor for the 4th Battalion, the Parachute Regiment. Dr. Keene has published numerous internal/

external MoD and NATO reports as well as award-winning academic journal articles, and is the author of *Threat Finance: Disconnecting the Lifeline of Organized Crime and Terrorism*. Dr. Shima holds an M.Phil. in defence and security studies and graduated with honors in Business Studies, and a Ph.D. in international criminal law.

SUMMARY

In the current age of economic austerity, there is increasing pressure for the military in the United States and the United Kingdom (UK) to be streamlined, so as to be able to deliver more for less cost. This requires a whole new approach to warfare supported by additional skill sets, many of which are not currently readily or widely available within the military. These skills have become even more vital in the current security environment of networked global insecurities. As such, there is a need for the military not only to re-establish lost skills, but to develop new skills to enhance its ability to tackle the emerging security threats of the 21st century.

One way in which such skills shortages can be addressed is by accessing existing skill sets within the civilian workforce, which can be achieved through the recruitment of reservists. Reservists have been utilized not only by the U.S. Army, but also by numerous armies around the world, including the UK, where the reliance on Reservists has increased significantly in recent years. However, recent reviews carried out by the UK Ministry of Defence (MoD) identified a range of deficiencies highlighting the need for UK Reserve Forces to be modernized so that they can be utilized in a manner that is efficient, cost effective, and sustainable. Consequently, this monograph explores the various types of reservist roles and deployment options, as well as factors that are both detrimental and beneficial to the recruitment, retention, and use of Reservists, highlighting areas where the UK experience is of potential relevance to the U.S. Army's future options.

It is recognized that U.S. Reserve Forces are bigger, better funded, and more integrated with the Regular

Army compared to the UK. However, there are also many similarities between the two forces, such that the cross-fertilization of experiences can be of mutual benefit. For example, both the United States and the UK have suffered the effects of the economic downturn, one side effect has been the need to cut defense spending. As a result, each has recently made a decision to reduce the size of its Regular Army, compensating for the reduction by a greater reliance on the use of Reserve Forces. This decision has met with criticism in both the United States and the UK, with many questioning the extent to which reservists can be used to "replace" regular forces. Some have expressed serious concern regarding over-reliance on Reserve Forces, viewing this as potentially weakening and endangering defense capabilities as a whole.

On the other hand, others have argued that such concerns are not based on evidential data, but instead on prejudice, and that it is the culture of the Regular Army that needs to be addressed. This debate has encouraged further research and analysis into numerous aspects of Reserve Forces so that an assessment can be made as to the validity of the concerns expressed. In order to contribute to this assessment, the aim of this monograph is to highlight the lessons learned by the UK Reserve Forces, both in terms of successes and challenges, as well as to explore the feasibility of achieving the proposals set out by *Future Reserves 2020*. This may be useful for the United States moving forward as the need to cut defense spending further is likely, and the UK may serve as a good model of how to operate with a smaller budget. The assessments are intended to assist the United States to consider the successful elements of the UK model and its reform program, while avoiding the errors and unintended detrimental consequences identified.

One case study, with a focus on the use of reservists with specialist skills, examines the use of medical professionals such as doctors. Another examines the use of subject matter experts through the recently established Specialist Group Military Intelligence (SGMI) unit, whose principal strength is its ability to utilize the breadth of Reservist capability to provide a depth of expertise to the Field Army, defense, and the wider government that would be both uneconomical and untimely to develop within a regular unit; and prohibitively expensive to contract from the private sector. In addition, negative outcomes of reform processes in the UK are highlighted, in particular the disastrous effect on recruitment and retention of outsourcing key programs to the private sector. The analysis provided leads to recommendations to enhance the overall capability and utility of the U.S. Armed Forces; better harness the talents and the volunteer ethos of the U.S. population; provide the U.S. Army with better integration with, and understanding by, the society from which its manpower is drawn; and improve the cost-effectiveness of defense.

ENDNOTES

1. In the UK system, DCEs are nongovernment civilians who are available for deployment, often at short notice, for assignments in countries affected by or at risk of violent conflict. They are part of the CSG, which is a pool of skilled individuals who are deployed to fragile and conflict-affected countries to assist the UK Government in addressing instability.

2. The Stabilisation Unit is an interdepartmental agency of the UK government, jointly owned by the Foreign and Commonwealth Office, the Department for International Development, and the MoD.

THE EFFECTIVE USE OF RESERVE PERSONNEL IN THE U.S. MILITARY: LESSONS FROM THE UNITED KINGDOM RESERVE MODEL

INTRODUCTION

During the Cold War, the U.S. and United Kingdom (UK) militaries possessed robust expertise on the culture and decisionmaking processes of potential adversaries, in the form of numerous linguists and foreign area officers whose purpose was, in part, to study foreign countries and to prepare for possible deployments to various continents. However, due to the past 10 years of constant operational deployments, this critical capability has been diminished. In the existing security environment, such international relations capability is essential not only in understanding the developing threat environment, but to serve as an early warning system and means of identifying issues and problems before any potential need for military intervention arises.

In addition, there is a need for the military to develop and sustain a new range of skill sets in order to better understand and tackle today's highly technical, globalized, and complex security threat environment. To keep up to speed and attempt to stay ahead of emerging threats, the deployment of a new breed of soldier who is a specialist/subject matter expert (SME) in a range of necessary disciplines is vital. As such, there is an immediate need for both the U.S. and British Army to address existing skills shortages, both in terms of the re-establishment of "foreign relations" skills which have diminished over the last decade, as well as developing new additional skills essential for the battlefield of the 21st century.

1

One solution is for the military to better access and utilize existing relevant civilian skills through the recruitment of Reservists who have developed the necessary skill sets outside the military environment. Reservists are able to provide additional capacity as well as to make available specialist expertise which would not be practical or cost effective to maintain as a regular capability. In recognition of these challenges, the UK Reserve Forces are in the process of undergoing a radical change in an attempt to professionalize and make better use of their Reservists.

UK VERSUS U.S. RESERVE FORCES

U.S. Reserve Forces are larger, better funded, and represent a larger ratio of the whole force compared to the UK Reserve Forces. For example, the U.S. Army Reserves and the U.S. Army National Guard form 20 percent[1] and 32 percent,[2] respectively, of total Army Personnel, representing a combined total of just over half of the U.S. Army, compared to the proposed 27 percent[3] which the UK is hoping to achieve. The U.S. Reserve Forces are also better integrated with their regular counterpart, in that the "Total Force" concept[4] was adopted shortly after the end of large-scale U.S. military involvement in Vietnam in 1973,[5] whereas the concept is only just in the process of being established in the UK. Nevertheless, there are numerous similarities, especially in terms of challenges that both countries face. For example, both have suffered the effects of the economic downturn resulting in the need to cut defense spending. As a result, both the United States and the UK have recently decided to reduce the size of their Regular Army.

U.S. Army Chief of Staff General Ray Odierno announced in June 2013 that the Regular Army would downsize the number of Brigade Combat Teams from 45 to 33, reducing the number of Soldiers from 570,000 to 490,000 by 2017.[6] In addition, U.S. Defense Secretary Chuck Hagel has recommended shrinking forces even further, to between 440,000 and 450,000, making the total cut in personnel between 120,000 and 130,000.[7] Similarly in the UK, British forces are undergoing a 20 percent reduction in Regular Army numbers from 102,000 to 82,000, to be implemented between 2010 and 2018.[8] However, this cut has been compensated by the proposed increase and better use of Reserve Forces. In addition, the UK's Territorial Army was rebranded as the "Army Reserve" in an attempt to move away from its previous ambiguous reputation as part-time soldiers or "weekend warriors," and adopt a more professional image to reflect its actual role and function.

In the United States, although the budget for its Reserve Forces has been reduced, the Department of Defense's (DoD) 2012 strategic guidance stated that the impact of the defense cuts on Reserve Forces and the National Guard would be minimal. Furthermore, General Odierno confirmed in January 2012 that the decision to cut the active force by 80,000 Soldiers would place even greater reliance on the National Guard and Reserves than ever before.[9]

There are four key arguments supporting the use of Reserves.

Rationale for the Use of Reserves.

Skill Set:

The world today faces a diverse range of security risks resulting in strategic uncertainties. These challenges can only be countered by an agile military organization with appropriate skill sets to meet these challenges. In addition, the fast evolving nature of the threat environment is such that it is unrealistic that all of the necessary skills could be available on a full-time basis. As such, it makes sense to utilize civilian talent and skills if and when required through the use of Reservists.

Deployability:

Reserve Forces are deployable. This is particularly relevant in the context of specialist knowledge (See "Specialists" section on succeeding pages. Case study on Specialist Group Military Intelligence) where an SME is required. Such expertise can often be found within civilian government employees, but these are not a deployable resource.

Cost:

Affordability is often a dominant argument put forward in relation to the use of Reserve Forces. There are considerable cost implications to developing additional specialist skill sets required in-house. In addition to the cost of training days payable to the Soldier, the cost of hiring specialist teaching staff, as well as providing facilities such as classrooms, training materials, travel, accommodation, and subsistence needs to be considered. On the other hand, as "specialist/expert" Reservists have already developed the necessary skills, all that is required is the provision of remedial training to enable skills to be transferred for use in the military environment. This not only results in considerable savings but also presents excellent value in terms of continued use of that expertise.

For example, in the UK, a clinical toxicologist takes over 10 years to train and would usually bill at a daily rate of £1,200 ($2,000),[10] reflecting the availability of approximately 20 suitably qualified individuals nationally. The same individual recruited as a Reservist at the rank of staff officer (SO2), usually an O-4 equivalent, would instead be paid a daily rate of £91.81 ($155),[11] representing a considerable cost advantage compared to the full rate the military would have to pay if the individual were employed as an outside consultant.

In terms of running costs of the unit as a whole, the cost of Reserve Forces is considerably lower compared with Regular Forces. For example, in the UK, a Reserve unit of comparable size to its regular counterpart costs approximately 20 percent of the latter's manpower bill when not mobilized. When mobilized, a Reserve unit costs 10-15 percent less than its mobilized regular counterpart.[12]

Political:

Popular opinion continues to play a key role in warfare. "All warfare requires the political support and consensus of the people in whose name it is waged."[13] As such, societal buy-in is key. Reserve Forces can be seen as a gateway for the military to engage with many different elements of society, including businesses who may be the employers of Reservists, as well as their family and friends. Supporting and championing Reservists enables society to become more engaged with matters relating to defense. This is a view shared by the United States, which forms the basis of the Total Force Concept. General Creighton Abrams intertwined the structure of the three components of the Army in such a way as to make extended operations impossible, without the involvement of both the Army National Guard and the Army Reserve. One interpretation of General Abrams' intent in doing so was to ensure that no U.S. President should be able to take the United States (and more specifically the U.S. Army) to war without the support of the American people.[14]

UK RESERVE FORCES

Thirty years ago, the UK's Armed Forces were designed to fight a conventional war of national survival. The principal role of the Reserve Forces was to provide mass reinforcements to help counter the Soviet threat, and there was little political appetite for their use in any other contingency, such as the Falklands Conflict in 1982.[15] However, the end of the Cold War led to the reduction in size of the Regular Forces, which in turn led to an increase in the use of Reserve Forces in operations such as the Balkans, Iraq, Afghanistan, and Libya.[16] Since April 1, 2003, 26,219 UK Reservists (army, navy, and air force) have deployed globally, as well as within the UK, in a variety of roles ranging from infantryman to intelligence analyst.

Recent examples include Operation HERRICK in Afghanistan, Operation TELIC in Iraq, and the London 2012 Olympic and Paralympic Games,[17] where

Reservists made up approximately 15 percent of Defense's contribution to safety and security.[18] At their peak in 2004, Reservists made up 20 percent of UK forces in Iraq and 12 percent in Afghanistan.[19] The UK Army Reserve (formerly known as the Territorial Army [TA]), produced almost one in 10 soldiers who served in Afghanistan, a large proportion of which were medical staff. A number of Reservists have been decorated, and at least 27 have lost their lives.[20] As a result, the image of the TA as somewhere people go to "play" soldier has begun to diminish in recent years. However, the stigma attached to being "part-time" soldiers remains and needs to be addressed, as rebranding alone is unlikely to achieve the necessary shift in perception.

UK RESERVIST CATEGORIES

In recognition of differing circumstances and skill sets, several categories of Reservists exist within the UK. There are two principal categories of Reservists, the Volunteer Reserves and the Ex-Regular Reserves.

Volunteer Reserves.

Volunteer Reserves are members of society who accept an annual training commitment and a liability to be mobilized to deploy on operations. They comprise the Royal Naval Reserve, the Royal Marines Reserve, the Army Reserve, and the Royal Auxiliary Air Force. Reservists typically attend training on a part-time basis throughout the year, including an Annual Camp which runs for approximately 2 weeks.[21] Volunteer Reserves are paid at the same rates as regular personnel and become eligible for an annual tax exempt bounty payment on completion of a specified amount of training per year.[22]

As Volunteer Reserves are at a known level of readiness, they are usually the first Reservists called on for operations.[23] In addition, a Volunteer Reservist can sign a contract to undertake a full-time role for a set period of time (Full-Time Reserve Service), a part-time or intermittent additional role (Additional Duties Commitment or an increased liability for call-out when they have skills which may be needed at short notice (High Readiness Reserves [HRR]).

Ex-Regular Reservists.

Ex-regular Reservists are former members of the Regular Forces who retain a liability to be called up for service. On completion of the period of liability for recall, all become members of the Long-Term Reserve up to the age of 55, or on completion of 18 years in the Regular Reserve. The Long-Term Reserve may only be recalled for national danger, great emergency, or attack on the UK. In general, ex-regular Reservists have only been called upon to support routine operations if they have volunteered or when volunteer Reservists have not been available.[24]

High Readiness Reserves.

HRR were introduced in the Reserve Forces Act 1996 (RFA 96) and are drawn from both Ex-Regular Reserves and Volunteer Reserves. They comprise individuals who may be trained to a higher standard and are available for military service at an agreed minimum notice, for which they receive an annual payment. The agreement of the employer is required before an individual can be accepted as an HRR.[25]

Sponsored Reserves.

Sponsored Reserves (SRs) were created by RFA 96 in order to allow certain support tasks to be carried out by trained professionals. They are members of a civilian workforce who are required to join the volunteer or ex-regular Reserves as a condition of a contract, which their civilian employer has entered into with the MoD to provide a capability under normal conditions as well as on operations. Generally the MoD uses SRs to fill capability gaps which they wish to control.

Among others, a number of discrete contracts have been awarded for Heavy Equipment Tank Transportation, STUFT shipping,[26] and the UK Meteorological Office.[27] Over 2,000 personnel hold SR status across a range of military capabilities as diverse as fulfilling the UK's strategic sealift[28] requirement,[29] provision of aviation weather services to the Royal Air Force (RAF) and Army Air Corps, advising on environmental factors affecting operations,[30] and meeting the Army's need for the transportation of heavy equipment.

CURRENT STATUS OF THE UK RESERVE FORCES

In November 2012, the Independent Commission to Review the UK's Reserve Forces published its findings in a Green Paper[31] having reached four main conclusions. The first was that the UK Reserve Forces were in decline; second, that the role of the Reservist needed to be modernized; third, that the potential of Reserve Forces had not been fully harnessed; and fourth, that they were not used in a cost-effective manner.[32] A public consultation followed, prompting over 3,000 responses, which in turn led to the publication of a UK Government white paper[33] setting out the future relationships MoD seeks with Reservists, their employers, and society.[34] The paper also introduced the Future Reserves 2020 (FR20) Programme as part of the wider Transforming Defence campaign that aims to transform the UK Armed Forces and deliver Future Force 2020.[35]

FR 2020 PROGRAMME

FR20 stipulates that by 2020, a greater proportion of the overall Defense effort will be contributed by the Reserves. In recognition of the decline in morale among existing Reservists, coupled with the declining trend in recruitment, FR20 proposes to "revitalize" the role of Reservists through better training and improved clarity of purpose, coupled with better integration with Regular Forces. In addition, the introduction of new legislation to better enable mobilization was proposed, and the TA was renamed the "Army Reserve," to reflect the major changes to its role and its integral place as part of the Whole Force concept.[36] Furthermore, the importance of the relationship between the Reservist and their families and employers, as well as society as a whole, in terms of both recruitment and retention, was recognized. As a result, the program aims to further develop these relationships with the aim of achieving further buy-in and support through the introduction of the following measures.

Family.

Recent studies have shown that families play a key role in the recruitment and retention of Reservist personnel and that family support is the biggest pre-dictor of retention and readiness of Reservists.[37] Reservist pay, although not a primary incentive for Reservists themselves, has been identified as playing an important role in "sweetening" family relationships, as it was frequently used as a negotiation tool to allow the Reservist to continue his or her service. For example, Reservist pay was often presented as "extra income" which could be used to pay for family holidays and home improvements, benefitting the family as a whole.[38] This is of particular relevance in the UK's high taxation, low disposable income societal environment, but similar factors could be expected to affect U.S. Reservists from lower income brackets.

In recognition of the importance of pay as an incentive for both enrollment and continued service, the total pay package for UK Reservists was recently made more attractive. For example, the annual leave entitlement was introduced in April 2013, amounting to approximately 1 day's paid leave for every 10 training days completed. This is paid in addition to the current annual leave awarded for time on deployment, as well as the annual tax-free bounty.[39] The program rewards Reservists with high attendance, providing an incentive to continue their commitment year after year.

In addition, in an attempt to encourage retention of Reserve personnel on a long-term basis, pensions for Reservists were introduced for the first time. As of April 2015, when the new Armed Forces pension program comes into play, Reservists will accrue pension entitlements for time spent training as well as when mobilized. Other new financial incentives include the Reservist Award which, in some circumstances, provides for payments to make up the difference between civilian earnings and military salary when a Reservist is mobilized to ensure that the Reservist is not financially disadvantaged by mobilization.[40]

Employers.

The white paper also recognized the contribution made by employers of Reservists, resulting in the proposed introduction of a financial incentive of an additional monthly payment of £500 for small- and medium-sized enterprises when an employee is mobilized.[41] In addition, FR20 recommended the use of nonfinancial incentives such as a "kitemark-type"[42] award for supportive employers,[43] to provide appropriate recognition of the contribution those employers make.[44]

However, these changes do not adequately address concerns expressed by employers in relation to employee absence, which has been compared to maternity leave. In the UK, statutory maternity leave is 52 weeks,[45] accompanied by statutory maternity pay, which is paid up to 39 weeks.[46] In addition, paternity pay and leave is also available by law, albeit for a shorter duration of time.[47] One difference between absence due to maternity leave and military deployment is the notice period given to employers. Maternity leave typically starts with 4 to 6 months' notice, whereas military deployment can take place with a typical 1 to 3 months of advance warning. Consultation with employers highlighted that this shorter timescale was problematic as it makes it more difficult to make arrangements to provide cover during the employee's absence. A further difference is in relation to risk, as the possibility of the employee not returning at the expected time due to medical reasons, or not at all, is considerably higher. The loss of a member of staff for such long periods of time (temporary or permanent) is even harder for small- and medium-sized enterprises to accommodate, particularly if the employee concerned is highly skilled and hard to replace.[48]

At the same time, the consultations also revealed that many employers acknowledged the potential value that Reservists bring to their organization, in terms of additional skills developed in the form of leadership, people management, and initiative skills, which benefit the civilian employer. This was felt to be particularly relevant in the modern workplace, where academic qualifications alone are no longer deemed adequate, with employers increasingly seeking individuals with proven workplace skills such as team working, leadership, and effective communications.[49] Furthermore, a recent study conducted for MoD and endorsed by the UK's Chartered Management Institute, found that during a typical year, a Reservist gained skills from military training that would cost £8,327 ($14,156) for their civilian employers to buy.[50]

However, the majority of Reservists consulted reported that their role as a Reservist was at best tolerated by their employers, with the potential to damage career progression, especially if there was a high probability that they would be mobilized. As a result, most had downplayed their role as a Reservist or had avoided mentioning the subject at all to their employers or colleagues. This was particularly true of individuals in positions of seniority who were expected to have a high commitment to their role, and were often required to work long, demanding hours. Furthermore, many employers were likely to regard the Reservist's military commitments as being in direct conflict with their ability to contribute fully to their civilian role.

As such, more work is needed to resolve these issues, especially if the army is to utilize resources from the high skilled end of the market.

SKEPTICISM OVER FR20

Although proposals put forward by FR20 have been well received by many Reservists, considerable skepticism also exists as to whether they are achievable. The UK's National Audit Office, a government oversight body, concluded in a highly critical report entitled *Army 2020* that there was no evidence that "the feasibility of increasing the number of trained Reserves within the planned timescale, needed to provide the required capability, was robustly tested." The report also warned that the proposed changes in the new Army structure come with significant further risks, which if not mitigated "could significantly affect value for money and the Army's ability to achieve its objectives."[51]

The report found that "The Department [MoD] did not test whether increasing the trained strength of the Army Reserve to 30,000 was feasible" and that "the Department's recruitment targets for Reserves are not underpinned by robust planning data."[52] Indeed, as noted by Professor Vince Connelly of Oxford Brookes University,[53] any feasibility study may have been irrelevant:

> the final figure of 30K was actually imposed on the Army by the FR20 Independent Commission and… there was no choice about that figure at all. The Army was given the figure of 30k once [the UK Government] accepted the FR20 report.[54]

Although the main purpose of the restructuring is to reduce cost, the findings warn that "reducing the size of the Army will not alone deliver the financial savings required," and that "greater reliance on Reserves will help the Department make savings but may lead to increased costs for HM Treasury," an apparent paradox explained by the UK's system where the MoD pays for soldiers in peacetime, but Treasury — central Government finance — pays for "wartime costs," including the mobilization of Reserves. In particular, "the Department did not fully assess the value for money of its decision to reduce the size of the Army."[55]

What is of additional concern is that the Regular Army is ahead of its target to reduce its uniformed personnel to 82,500 by 2018 and deliver the staffing savings required by its reduced budget, but at the same time, the trained strength of the Army Reserve, which is intended to compensate for this, has not increased since April 2012 and the "recruitment of Reserve and regular soldiers is behind the requirement set by the Army for 2013-14."[56] The report also highlights that "The Department failed to provide Information and Communication Technology (ICT), infrastructure critical to the success of the Army's Recruiting Partnering Project with [outsourcing contractor] Capita," and consequently that "the Department's failure to enable the setting up of new recruitment software has impacted on recruitment activities and increased costs."[57]

These concerns over the ability to recruit and retain the additional number of Reservists stipulated are widespread, especially among currently serving Reservist personnel.[58] Furthermore, even if the proposed numbers are achieved, many also question whether future Reserve Forces will be able to sufficiently bolster the reduced Regular Force, not only in terms of numbers, but capability.[59]

RECRUITMENT AND RETENTION

Many believe that it is unrealistic to achieve the proposed growth from a trained strength of approximately 20,000[60] to 30,000 by 2018.[61] The concern is widespread and valid, given the declining trend in recruitment reported in recent years. For example, the number of volunteer Reserves (both trained and untrained, to include officers and other ranks) was 34,730 in 2003. This figure fell to 30,220 in 2009 and has steadily declined year after year to reach 26,500 in 2013.[62] Some UK media reporting, considered misleading by MoD insiders, has highlighted that the Army Reserves/TA are in "serious decline in terms of numbers, capability and morale" and that "current forecasts see the TA ageing and reducing to potentially unsustainable levels by 2015."[63]

However, Professor Connelly is optimistic that it would be possible to increase recruitment and points out that the decline can be attributed to ongoing manning challenges resulting from decisions made during the previous decade of sustained underfunding.

> Lots of TA units [have] actually shrunk in terms of the numbers they could recruit. . . . This reduction in posts primarily fell on the top end of the rank pyramid so that SNCO's and officers were squeezed out of orbats and so left. The number of TA staff posts also diminished over this period in certain areas. There seems to be a collective forgetting of these various measures over the years.[64]

An additional critical factor is that many Reservists believe the recent increase of mandatory training days

(MTDs) from 27 to 40 is not only unrealistic, given the demands of their career and personal commitments, but will result in serving members leaving, as well as make the recruitment of new Reservists more difficult.[65] In addition, the "one-size-fits-all" approach of setting a standard number of MTDs was heavily criticized. Some felt that while the increase to 40 MTDs would be welcomed by units such as the Officer Training Corps (OTC), others were already struggling to meet the 27-day requirement. The OTC consists of university students in full-time education, with long holiday periods where they are actively looking for paid work. As such, they not only have the time to attend training days, but are likely to try to maximize time spent with the OTC, as their pay as a Reservist is likely to be an important or even sole source of income.

In comparison, Reservists who are doctors or senior managers of an organization are highly paid but typically work demanding hours and already often struggle to meet the former 27-MTD requirement. Here, time is more valuable than pay, and as a result many forego their tax free annual bounty.[66] However, the inability to attend training days does not mean that they are less capable. This is especially true of medical practitioners such as doctors, who are practicing their trade in their civilian career on a daily basis.

RESERVE VERSUS REGULAR DEBATE

A further concern relates to whether Reservists, even when they are able to meet the training requirements, are capable of replacing Regular soldiers. A succession of planning decisions in the UK which called for reducing its regular troop numbers from

102,000 to 82,000, and attempting to replace the 20,000 regular troops with 30,000 Reservists has been met with criticism.[67] Despite planned investment of £1.8 billion (B) (U.S.$3.06B) over 10 years to enhance the capability and strength of Reserve Forces and better integrate them with the Regular Army,[68] many critics remain concerned about the impact of replacing a full-time soldier with a part-time Reservist.[69] According to one former soldier who served in the Regular Army: "We now have far too few people to do the role. We're relying too heavily on the TA or Reservists, as they've tried to rebrand them. And it's not working."[70]

This is a view that is shared by many. Similar concerns with respect to the ability of Reserves to perform to the necessary standards have also been raised in the United States. For example, Colonel Ted Spain, deployed to Iraq as the commander of the 18th Military Police Brigade in 2003, believes that the decision to deploy Army Reserve Officer Brigadier General Janis Karpinski to command the military police unit at the Abu Ghraib Prison was one of the key U.S. mistakes made during the Iraq war.[71]

In addition, *Army Quadrennial Defense Review* director Major General John Rossi has also recently questioned aspects of the National Guard's combat performance since September 11, 2001 (9/11).[72] These views were shared by retired U.S. Army Reserves Colonel Patrick Allen[73] who observed during his 21 years of service that: ". . . Regular soldiers are almost always better qualified than the National Guard or Reservists, due to the differences in the number of training hours as well as resources such as training ammunition."[74]

At the same time, Colonel Allen also highlighted that Reservists with specialist skill sets, who perform similar or identical roles in their civilian occupation, often perform better in that role compared to their Regular military counterpart. This is predominantly because these individuals benefit from military training as well as, not instead of, civilian training. In addition, they have developed their knowledge and trade through practical/operational experience both in and out of uniform.

Giving the examples of the use of fuel truck operators and cyber experts, Allen argues that one advantage of the Reserves and the National Guard is that when specialists are required, the existence of already trained personnel means that the Army does not need to invest in training from scratch. In other words, remedial training can be provided to get the Reserve and Guard Units to the desired level of training much more quickly than starting from no unit at all.

The same situation applies in the UK where Reserve personnel undergo intensive mobilization training prior to deployment. According to former infantry officer Major (Ret.) Anthony Ball, this is adequate to enable soldiers to reach the necessary level of proficiency equal to that of their Regular counterparts. Ball, who has 20 years of service in both the Regular Army and the Reserves, argues that although there may be some Reservists who fail to come up to scratch, this is equally true of soldiers in the Regular Army.

Overall, recent operational tours have shown that the performance of Reservists has not been an issue, and that they have worked well alongside the Regular Army once they have had an opportunity to prove their professionalism and capabilities in the field. However, despite evidence of the ability of Reserve Forces to perform satisfactorily in operations, there continues to be a belief that Reservists do not possess the same level of professionalism and skills. The subject deserves closer examination to determine whether this is a justifiable concern, or mere prejudice that needs to be overcome.

PERCEPTION OF THE PART-TIME PROFESSIONAL

There is a perception among the Regular Army that Reserve Forces cannot be regarded as fellow professionals. This arises because the full time element of the Army defines who is a professional by judgment against full-time norms. For example, an Army professional is someone who demonstrates a strong commitment and 24/7 availability to the organization. Thus, individuals who do not show they work full-time hours and are not available 24/7 (i.e., who are part-time) will be seen as not wholly committed and so will be perceived as less professional in their status, no matter how well they may perform in their roles.[75] However, this view is not unique to the armed forces.[76] Full-time employees in other professions such as the police also struggle to view their part-time colleagues as true professionals.[77] This is also reported to be the case with respect to professions where the initial training or education has been equivalent. Examples include doctors, nurses and accountants, where the employee have reduced their hours from full-time to part-time.[78]

Peter Quinn, Research Fellow in Military Sciences at British defense and security think-tank Royal United Services Institute (RUSI),[79] goes as far as to dismiss the fundamental principles behind the Whole Force Concept, arguing that the implication of the "integrated" and "single force" command slogans, that Reservists are equivalent to their regular counterparts, is a myth. Quinn believes that regular capabilities cannot be replicated on a part-time basis, and compares the Reservists 40-MTDs to the regulars' 223 annual working days. He further argues that ". . . those who claim otherwise discredit the professionalism of regulars and place unrealistic expectations on Reservists."[80]

There is clearly a valid argument that, if an individual has received less training than another in an equivalent position, that the ability of that individual to perform will be less than his or her better trained counterpart. The argument becomes stronger if the training provided is inferior. However, although this may be the case in some Reservist roles, this is not true in all cases. Furthermore, one "Reserve" training day does not necessarily equate to one "Regular" working day. For example, the Reserve training day is generally more intense, and, unlike regular soldiers, many Reservists are required to complete various tasks such as personal administration relating to the military, physical fitness training, and coursework preparation on their own unpaid time, outside reported "training" hours.

At the same time, the key differential between the Army Reserve and Regular Army is that for most Reservists, the army is not his or her sole career. In fact, many do not view their role as a Reservist as a career. Although there is considerable evidence to illustrate that Reservists are capable of performing well, and are able to contribute significantly to the overall Defense effort, it must also be recognized that the Reservist's main priority is likely to be his or her day job. It is perhaps this fact that will always differentiate Reserve Forces from the Regular Military. Nevertheless, the following case studies illustrate the valuable contribution that Reserve Forces currently make and will continue to make for the foreseeable future, which needs to be recognized.

CASE STUDIES

Case Study 1: The Medical Corps.

In the British Army, core health and medical services are provided by the Royal Army Medical Corps (RAMC). The majority of RAMC Reservists ordinarily work for the National Health Service (NHS) in the UK. Currently there are over 2,000 NHS staff serving as Reservists.[81] The NHS as an employer is a supporter of Reserve Forces, making the recruitment and retention of Reservists less challenging. Furthermore, as their "day" job is to work in the medical services, typically as doctors or nurses, the argument that they are less professional or experienced compared to their regular counterpart cannot hold true. Despite this, Medical Corps Reservists deployed in Iraq and Afghanistan reported receiving considerable skepticism from their Regular counterparts.

The view that field hospitals run by Reservists were somehow inferior to those run by regulars came not only from regular RAMC personnel, but also from the injured soldiers who were admitted into those hospitals.[82] But despite their initial apprehension on learning that the Reservists were mostly NHS staff in their "day" jobs, the injured soldiers soon reported that they felt that they were in even better hands. This was because many viewed NHS care to be better than that of the military. This resulted partly from the general positive image of the NHS in British society, but also from the soldiers' belief that by receiving both civilian and military training and education, the Reservists benefited from superior training and experience and a wider breadth of knowledge.

In this situation, while the doctors and nurses may only be part-time in terms of their military commitments, they are full-time medical professionals, and so the argument that they are somehow less professional than their regular counterparts clearly does not apply. Furthermore, even when the Reservist's main career was not in medicine, it is questionable as to whether he or she was less skilled than a regular Medic/Combat Medical Technician (CMT). For example, some Reservists who serve as Medics in a noncommissioned role often hold highly skilled jobs in their civilian life. Some are senior managers in their own professions, who are not only well-qualified academically, but have a broad range of practical management skills which can be used effectively in their role as an Army Medic.

Specialists.

The medical profession is not the only field where specialist civilian skills can be utilized by the military. Military Intelligence is another example where specialists play a key role. At the heart of intelligence is analysis.[83] The importance for the analyst to not only possess general analytical capabilities, but also in-depth specialist knowledge, was acknowledged in the UK Government's Butler Report[84] in 2004:

> Analysis can be conducted only by people expert in the subject matter — a severe limitation when the topic is as specialised as biological warfare or uranium enrichment, or the internal dynamics of terrorist cells or networks[85]

The Butler report further cautioned that a "special danger here can be the failure to recognise just what particular expertise is required."[86] In other words, it requires an individual with specialist knowledge to understand the problem in order to be able to recommend additional expertise required. This observation highlights the importance of involving specialists in the operational role of the headquarters element to ensure that any force generated has the correct experts. Against this background, the UK's 2010 *Strategic Defence and Security Review* recognized both the importance of "understanding" and the cost-benefits that could be realized through the use of Reservists.[87]

Reserve Forces have the flexibility to be mobilized and deployed, unlike their civilian counterparts in government service. This has resulted in the birth of the concept of the SGMI, a deployable cadre of deep specialists that can provide technical expertise across a wide spectrum of disciplines in support of both national and operational objectives.[88]

Case Study 2: Specialist Group Military Intelligence.

In recognition that "Analysis can be conducted only by people expert in the subject matter,"[89] the formation of the Specialist Group Military Intelligence (SGMI) was announced in a UK Ministerial Statement on Reserves in 2013. The Group's remit is to extend the capability available to defense forecasting, intelligence, and understanding through cost-effective access to the breadth and depth of specialist intelligence, scientific, and technical expertise available through the Army Reserve. Its work falls under the banner of technical intelligence (TECHINT) which is defined as:

intelligence concerning foreign [or nonstate actor] technological developments, and the performance and operational capabilities of foreign [or nonstate actor] materiel, which have or may eventually have a practical application for military purposes.[90]

Although such a capability was developed during World War II, this had lapsed, and in recent times until the formation of SGMI, the British Army had no central repository of specialist intelligence personnel.

SGMI is an independent Army Reserve unit under the operational command and administrative control of 1 Military Intelligence Brigade, but is expected to migrate to the Intelligence, Surveillance and Reconnaissance Brigade when this formation is stood up. The Unit will eventually consist of three pillars: Technical Intelligence Specialists Organisation (TISO); Human Domain Intelligence Specialists (HDIS), and Regional and Thematic Intelligence Specialists (RTIS). A headquarters element will also be established to provide the command and staff elements to enable tasking and force generation.

Technical Intelligence Staff Organisation: The Technical Intelligence Staff Organisation (TISO) will evolve directly from the existing Technical Intelligence Staff Officers pool. The brand name TISO will endure, although Officer will be changed to Organisation to reflect the inclusion of warrant officers for the first time. The new sections retain the traditional specialism of the former pool: materiel and personnel exploitation; weapons, ordnance, munitions and explosives (WOME); military systems and chemical, biological, radiation and nuclear. In addition, an infrastructure and environment section will be included to provide understanding of critical infrastructure. The new TISO will triple the size of the former pool with the distribution of manpower reflecting Defense priorities. As such, WOME, is likely to be the largest at present. In addition, the HDIS and RTIS pillars will enhance the capabilities of SGMI to provide expert coverage of disciplines not traditionally associated with TISO.

Human Domain Intelligence Specialists: The Human Domain Intelligence Specialists (HDIS) areas of expertise will include technical networks; social networks; governance (political "science" and economics) and human science (including ergonomics and psychology).

Regional and Thematic Intelligence Specialists: Regional and Thematic Intelligence Specialists (RTIS), the third pillar, is to have two regional sections to foreign area specialists. A thematic section will provide expertise in areas such as criminology, finance, narcotics, and terrorism. The composition of this section is likely to be highly flexible to reflect strategic and operational priorities.

The proposed composition of SGMI reflects an appreciation of the likely character of future conflict and the role that understanding will play in it.[91] Current UK doctrine notes that understanding, the foresight that arises from the application of judgment to situational analysis, in future conflict will be achieved through a deep appreciation of the human domain framework.[92] It is clear that specialist intelligence is a key enabler in delivering timely understanding of the future battle space and the new Reservist SGMI is well placed to provide this capability in a cost-effective and timely manner that would be unlikely to be provided through the regular Army or private sector. At the same time, it must be recognized that SGMI is currently in its early stages of development and faces a number of challenges which it must overcome if it is to fully realize its potential.

CHALLENGES

The future success of any of the specialist units in the Reserves depends upon their ability to identify and recruit suitably qualified personnel. Furthermore, they must do so without compromising on the quality of their specialist personnel, as so doing will result in a loss of credibility. As such, the following challenges need to be recognized and addressed.

Challenge 1: How Do You Find the Right Person?

The reputation of these units relies heavily on the credibility of the expert in the eye of the customer. This usually requires professional recognition at a national or international level. However, it is not always easy to determine the reputation of an expert if expertise does not already exist, making the assessment of the suitability of a candidate difficult. A starting point is to recruit individuals with a relevant higher degree from a reputable university, coupled with fellowship or chartered membership of a relevant professional body or a suitable employment record. The majority of serving officers in these roles already meet these criteria, and are either employed in a consultancy role outside the military, or in the case of medical specialists, usually within the NHS.

Challenge 2: How Do You Successfully Recruit that Individual?

Even when a suitable candidate is located, the next challenge is how to recruit that individual who is unlikely to be looking for additional work, especially if he or she is successful in their own career. As noted earlier, pay is not the primary motivator for Reservists. At the same time, all Reservists consulted stated that they would not serve without financial compensation. Furthermore, although the motivation for Reservists to join Reserve Forces varied from individual to individual, most agreed that they would not have joined if they felt that serving as a Reservist would damage their main career. This is even more relevant for potential recruits into units such as SGMI where there is a close overlap between the role and function of their main career and their work as a Reservist.

For example, if a business manager in civilian life is an infantryman, the two careers are quite separate. Apart from time needed for training and deployment on operations, the Reservist is likely to develop additional skills such as leadership, which he or she will bring back. As such, this is a positive relationship. However, if you have a SME in Terrorism, for example, their work as a Reservist has the potential of having a direct impact on their main career due to the similarity of the work.

One potential concern relates to professional status, which in turn is closely related to pay. As an SME, the daily rate is important, not so much in terms of the actual amount paid, but more as a reflection of your worth. In other words, the pay rate is an indicator of status used to demonstrate the level of professional recognition. For example, the résumé of an SME may indicate qualifications equivalent to the rank of Colonel in a civil service role. However, if that individual is recruited as a far lower rank, such as a Captain, the implication is that the individual is not a true expert.

Another concern is in relation to travel. If the SME is internationally recognized, it is likely that their work will require international travel, often at short notice. Existing military bureaucracy requires individuals to request and be granted authorization prior to international travel. This is not a realistic expectation as such a restriction will damage the SME's ability to carry out his or her main job, and as such, could well deter that individual from joining as a Reservist.

Challenge 3: Security Clearance.

A challenge relating to the recruitment of specialists is security clearance in those areas where higher level clearances may be required. Traditionally, recruitment of specialists was restricted to experienced staff officers with a specialist qualification who at the same time held developed vetting clearance (an approximate UK equivalent of top secret/sensitive compartmented information [TS/SCI] clearance). However, this becomes a real challenge if the specialism required is a Pashto[93] speaker with the Waneci[94] dialect who has an in-depth understanding of not only the language but the local culture, which must be current. As the individual will be working with sensitive material, he or she must be capable of obtaining the necessary security clearances. The first requirement for obtaining such security clearances is that the individual must be a British national.

However, the challenge is in finding an individual who has been born and bred in the UK with the necessary local knowledge and skills, who not only has the ability to translate, but the ability to fully appreciate the nuances of the language. There may be fluent speakers of Pashto trained by the military. However, the limitations of an individual with 1 year of training in Pashto and a short course on Afghan culture at the

Defence Centre for Languages and Culture must be understood. These individuals are typically used in operations as translators and are trained to be able to hold basic conversations with the local populace without offending them too much. However, what will be required from a specialist is an individual with a far more sophisticated knowledge of the language and culture. In other words, you need someone who is a native. This is not currently possible given the restrictions relating to security clearance, which the army needs to consider how to address.

Challenge 4: How Do You Retain the Expertise?

Even when a suitable candidate has been successfully recruited, the next potential challenge is retention. Recent studies and consultations have highlighted that wastage is at its highest between the period of enrollment and initial training. According to Professor Connelly, who conducted research into wastage of Reserve personnel, the patterns are similar to gym memberships. The initial period shortly after joining is important as this is where the new member is "trying out" the gym to access suitability. Any negative experiences during this period are likely to deter that individual from continuing his or her membership.

The same situation applies to Reservists, in that the impression of the army given at the initial stage, to include administrative procedures such as medicals, issuing of uniforms, and basic training, will have a profound impact on whether that recruit continues the training. Interviews conducted not only with staff from specialist National Reserve units, but also with infantry regiments and Medical Corps personnel, all indicated that this initial stage was a real problem, where they were struggling to maintain recruits. The reason provided by all consulted was administrative blunders and the poor quality of training, which had been outsourced in an effort to cut costs. Crucially, this is also reported to be the case for the Regular Army.[95] As such, the cost benefit of outsourcing needs to be assessed with extreme caution.

Dangers of Outsourcing.

The benefit of outsourcing as a means of controlling and minimizing cost is well established. There are examples (see section on Sponsored Reserves) where outsourcing has worked well. At the same time, the outsourcing of recruitment has been a disaster for the UK armed forces, to include the Regular Army. For example, the main objective of the UK's 10-year, £440 million (M) (U.S.$748M) deal to privatize recruitment was to enable a saving of £300 million (U.S.$510M). However, this has resulted in a sharp drop in the number of recruits. In October 2013, the Defense Correspondent for the UK's influential *Daily Telegraph* newspaper reported that: ". . . the Army is facing a recruitment crisis after a cost-cutting outsourcing deal resulted in the number of people joining up falling by more than a third."[96] Figures obtained by the newspaper showed that the number of people attending Army interviews and selection tests to be regular soldiers had fallen by 35 percent since Capita, a contracting and services corporation, had taken over recruitment. According to one senior infantry regiment source, "What this has done is completely erode an effective system. Although it delivers savings, it doesn't deliver a result."[97]

Just as in the Regular Army, within the Army Reserves numerous problems have arisen over the administration of new recruits as well as basic training, which has also been outsourced to a private contractor. According to one Staff Officer at 256 Field Hospital, "Outsourcing has been a nightmare and a total disaster. We've lost a lot of recruits who just had enough and decided not to proceed with their enrollment and basic training."[98]

Examples provided include a series of administrative blunders such as a new recruit turning up on a specified date and time to be issued his or her uniform, only to find that the relevant person in charge of issuing uniforms (from the outsourced company) was unavailable that day. Typically, the individual would be told to return on another day, which was problematic as appointments have to be made during normal working hours, requiring the recruit to take further time off work. While a recruit may be prepared to take one day off, repeated blunders eating into limited vacation time form an early impression that the organization they are in the process of joining lacks basic competence — enough in some cases for the recruit to withdraw their application altogether.[99]

Another commonly reported problem was difficulty in completing medical examinations, a prerequisite of the recruit being allowed to begin basic training. The process was reported to have become so cumbersome and time-consuming as a result of outsourcing, that many recruits were reported to have given up and decided not to continue with their service in the Reserves.

The same complaints were voiced by Reservists in all branches, whether in combat arms such as infantry or technical corps such as the RAMC, Intelligence, and so on. This highlights the need when considering outsourcing to focus on value for money as opposed to cost reduction alone.

CONCLUSIONS AND POLICY RECOMMENDATIONS

Given the on-going climate of economic austerity, the pressure to cut defense spending and achieve more for less cost is likely to continue into the foreseeable future. As a result, the use and reliance on Reserve Forces is likely to increase. The argument for the use of Reserve Forces is not only their affordability compared to Regular Forces, but also the ability to access relevant specialist skills which are currently either not widely available or entirely unavailable within the Regular Army. An added advantage is that Reservists serve as a gateway to wider society, enabling political buy-in for matters relating to defense through family, friends and employers of Reservists.

Cost Cutting Initiatives.

With on-going pressure to reduce defense spending, new cost reduction initiatives are likely to be of interest to the United States. Here, the UK may serve as a valid case study, as it has been able to carry out operations at a fraction of the U.S. budget. As such, the United States may look to the UK for other models, as well as to see how these initiatives have worked, in order to be able to make an assessment of the likelihood for success if similar measures are adopted in the United States. Outsourcing is a case in point where the United States may wish to explore why some measures have worked, while others have been counterproductive.

The U.S. defense budget is considerably bigger than the UK defense budget. As a result, the United States can afford a degree of personnel specialization which the UK simply cannot. This is exemplified at both unit and individual level, and is typified in the much broader range of Military Occupational Specialties (MOS) in the U.S. military, reflecting a narrower skill range within each MOS.[100] To take just one example, the U.S. Army's Career Management Field 94 "Electronic Maintenance and Calibrations" includes a multiplicity of MOS,[101] some specializing in single weapons systems. In the British Army, by contrast, these all come under the single multi-skilled "trade" of Electronics Artificer, which requires a higher education degree before progression to the rank of Staff Sergeant (E-7 equivalent). In short, a vastly smaller budget has resulted in soldiers being required to be far more omni-competent in the UK. The British skill and specialty distribution model may therefore provide a useful case study if continuing financial pressure forces the U.S. Army to examine new areas where costs can be reduced.

At the same time, the need to re-establish specialist human domain skills to address new security challenges applies to both the UK and the United States. As such, a re-establishment is a long-term process best achieved in the short term through the use of high level, internationally recognized SMEs recruited as Reservists. Here the SGMI model, which is still in its infancy, may prove useful. The United States is also better placed to effectively establish such a unit, as the U.S. budget is much less restrictive than that of the UK.

Nevertheless the limitations of the use of Reserve Forces must also be understood. Various challenges have been identified in this monograph in relation to the recruitment and retention of Reservists in the UK. In order to establish and maintain Reserve Forces that are fit for purpose to tackle the asymmetric threat environment of the 21st century, the UK needs to understand and tackle effectively the following specific challenges, which can also be translated to the U.S. planning environment:

Cultural Change.

The perception that Reserve Forces are inferior to the Regular Army is unlikely to change in the immediate future. In some cases, the perception is justified, as the training provided to some Reservists is inferior in terms of quality as well as quantity. However, this does not apply to specialists, where the perception is based on prejudice and lack of knowledge as to what the specialists are capable of and how they contribute to the defense effort.

Recommendations: In the case of Reservists with specialist skills, prejudice can be overcome by first establishing effective and fully operational specialist units; and second, by educating the Regular Army as to their purpose and function. Over time, these units could be seen as distinctive and valuable entities that bring value added to military operations. To achieve this, the recruitment of the right caliber of specialists is key. Counterintuitively, specialists should continue to be viewed as being different to the Regular Army, and their purpose being to fill a gap in skill sets as opposed to being part-time soldiers trying to fill a Regular Soldier's job. In relation to nonspecialists, prejudice can best be minimized through better training and integration with the Regular Army.

Training.

Although there are numerous examples to illustrate that Reserve Forces are capable of achieving the necessary standards of skills and professionalism, this can only be achieved when sufficient high quality training is provided.

Recommendation: Integrate training with Regular Forces where possible. This is best achieved when a Reserve Unit is structured so that it is directly in support of a parent Regular Unit. Currently, Regular Soldiers do not work evenings or weekends for training purposes, which is when the majority of the Reservists' training takes place. However, it is possible to integrate annual training camps and elements of trade courses to enable Reservists to appreciate what the required standard is in the Regular Army.

Furthermore, consideration should be given as to whether the Regular Army would be able to be more flexible with respect to their working hours. If Regular soldiers expected to work with Reservists were able to work 1 weekend every other month and therefore synchronize training elements with those Reservists, this would dramatically enhance the effort to integrate training. Existing negativity and prejudice on the part of the Regular Army toward the Reserve Forces at the present moment in time would make this difficult to achieve. However, efforts need to be made to overcome this.

Specialists.

The need for training does not apply to the same extent for specialists, such as doctors and SMEs. Here too, however, the ongoing stigma attached to being a

Reservist needs to be overcome. There are also numerous challenges relating to the service contracts of specialist personnel, such as rank, travel restrictions and security clearance, which need to be addressed.

Recommendation: Better integration with the Regular Army is necessary to enable the value of specialists to be better recognized. Standard Operating Procedures relating to security clearance, authorization for travel, and rank need to be re-examined to ensure that the flexibility is available to enable the highest caliber of personnel to be recruited and retained, and to ensure that the SME's career does not suffer as a result of his or her Reserve service.

Motivation — Incentives versus Disincentives.

With the exception of Reservists serving on a full-time basis, the Reservist is not economically reliant on the Army as they will have their own career outside the military. As such, the balance between incentives and disincentives plays a crucial role in the recruitment and retention of Reservists.

Recommendation: Efforts must be made to understand what the real incentives and disincentives are and to ensure that the former outweigh the latter. In other words, the motivation of Reservists, their families and employers needs to be better understood. In addition, a flexible approach is necessary to accommodate the needs of widely varying Reservists and the very different posts which they are intended to fill, and a one-size-fits-all approach to training must be avoided.

Dangers of Outsourcing.

In an attempt to control and cut costs, outsourcing to the private sector is likely to continue for the foreseeable future. However, lessons from the UK have shown that while some outsourcing programs have been successful, others have been nothing short of disastrous.

Recommendation: Based on the UK's experience, the single most important recommendation of this monograph is that cost must no longer be the only criterion for determining value. Instead, further consideration of the quality of output is essential. In addition, in each case, a feasibility study should be conducted to assess the likely outcome of outsourcing with reference to the individuals on the ground who will be impacted by the change and to senior military personnel, as well as the administrators and budget personnel currently consulted.

ENDNOTES

1. "For only 6 percent of the Army budget, the Army Reserve provides almost 20 percent of the Total Force." See *America's Army Reserve: A Life-saving and life-sustaining force for the Nation: 2013 Posture Statement*, Ft. Bragg, NC: U.S. Army Reserve, 2013, available from *www.usar.army.mil/resources/Media/ARPS_2013_6-6-13%20%282%29.pdf*, accessed May 10, 2014.

2. 2012 *National Guard Bureau Posture Statement: A great Value for America*, Washington, DC: National Guard Bureau, available from *www.nationalguard.mil/portals/31/Documents/PostureStatements /2012%20National%20Guard%20Bureau%20Posture%20Statement. pdf*, accessed May 10, 2014.

3. *Army 2020* envisages that the future UK army will be 112,000 by 2020, consisting of 82,000 Regular personnel and 30,000 Reservists. See *Library Standard Note Army 2020*, SN06396, London, UK, July 26, 2012.

4. The Whole Force concept involves treating the three components of the Army—the Regular Army, the Army National Guard, and the Army Reserve as a single force.

5. Gabriel Kolko, *Anatomy of a War: Vietnam, the United States and the Modern Historical Experience*, New York: Pantheon Books, 1985, pp. 457-461.

6. Paul D. Shrinkman, "Army to Cut 80,000 Soldiers," *US News*, June 23, 2013, available from *www.usnews.com/news/ articles/2013/06/25/army-to-cut-80000-soldiers-from-its-ranks-chief-says*, accessed May 13, 2014.

7. Andrew Feickert, "Army Drawdown and Restructuring: Background and Issues for Congress," Washington, DC: Congressional Research Service (CRS), February 28, 2014, available from *www.fas.org/sgp/crs/natsec/R42493.pdf*, accessed May 13, 2014.

8. Caroline Wyatt, "Has Britain's Defence Budget Been Cut Too Much?" BBC Defence Correspondent, *BBC News*, February 24, 2014, available from *www.bbc.co.uk/news/uk-26271018*, accessed May 13, 2014.

9. Lolita C. Baldor, "Army Chief Sees Greater Role for Guard and Reserves," *Norfolk Virginian-Pilot*, January 27, 2012. Taken from Feickert.

10. U.S. Dollar equivalent values use an exchange rate of £1 = $1.70, current as of July 1, 2014.

11. *Joint Service Publication 754, Tri-Service Regulations for Pay and Charges*, London, UK: Ministry of Defence, Ed. 18, April 1, 2013.

12. The Independent Commission to Review the United Kingdom's Reserve Forces, *Commission's Vision for the Reserve Forces in 2020*, London, UK: Ministry of Defence, July 2011, p. 11.

13. *Development, Concepts and Doctrine Centre (DCDC) Publication: Future Character of Conflict: Strategic Trends Programme*, London, UK: Ministry of Defence, February 1, 2010, p. 9, available from *www.da.mod.uk/colleges/jscsc/courses/RND/supporting-documents/*

20100201Future_Character_of_ConflictUDCDC_Strat_Trends_ 4.pdf/view, accessed May 7, 2014.

14. James Carafano: "Total Force Policy and the Abrams Doctrine: Unfulfilled Promise, Uncertain Future," No. 869, Washington, DC: The Heritage Foundation, April 18, 2005.

15. Chris Parry, *Down South: A Falklands War Diary*, London, UK: Viking Books, 2012.

16. The Independent Commission to Review the United Kingdom's Reserve Forces, p. 8.

17. *Use of Reservists during the Olympics*, London, UK: SaBRE publication, January 29, 2012, available from *www.sabre.mod.uk/ News/Olympics-2012#.U3SQMCjaNKU*, accessed May 15, 2014.

18. *Reserves in the Future Force 2020: Valuable and Valued*, London, UK: Ministry of Defence, White paper presented to Parliament by the Secretary of State for Defence by Command of Her Majesty, July 2013, p. 67.

19. The Independent Commission to Review the United Kingdom's Reserve Forces, p. 11.

20. Thomas Harding, "TA Troops 'Too Poorly Trained to Make Up for Army Cuts' The Reservists Who Replace Soldiers Made Redundant as Part of the Army Cuts Lack Commitment and Proper Training, Senior Military Figures Fear," *The Telegraph*, May 26, 2012, available from *www.telegraph.co.uk/news/uknews/ defence/9291338/TA-troops-too-poorly-trained-to-make-up-for- Army-cuts.html*, accessed May 7, 2014.

21. *TSP7 – UK Reserve Forces and Cadets April 1, 2013*, London, UK: Ministry of Defence, Defence Statistics (Tri Service), November 28, 2013, available from *https://www.gov.uk/government/ uploads/system/uploads/attachment_data/file/280401/2013.pdf*, accessed May 9, 2014.

22. A bounty is an annual tax free payment starting at £428, but rising with each year of qualifying service. Currently, the annual bounty after 5 years of service is £1,691. See *Territorial Army*

Rates of Pay, Bounties and Expenses, London, UK: MoD, April 2013, available from *www.army.mod.uk/documents/general/Rates_of_Pay_ TA.pdf,* accessed May 9, 2014.

23. *Reserves in the Future Force 2020: Valuable and Valued,* p. 16.

24. *Ibid.*

25. *Ibid.,* pp. 66-67.

26. STUFT (ship taken up from trade) is a civilian ship requisitioned for government use.

27. The RAF's Mobile Meteorological Unit (MMU) has been staffed since October 2000 by SRs of the Royal Auxiliary Air Force, who are otherwise civil service employees of the Met Office. The engineering support delivered by SERCO to the BAe 125 aircraft of the RAF's 32 (The Royal) Squadron came under an April 2001 agreement. See "Sponsored Reserves," the UK Defence Forum, FS56, available from *www.ukdf.org.uk/assets/downloads/FS56 SponsoredReserves.pdf,* accessed May 8, 2014.

28. The use of cargo ships for the deployment of military assets, such as weaponry, vehicles, military personnel, and supplies.

29. The Royal Navy's Strategic Sealift Capability, of six new two roll-on/roll-off (ro-ro) vessels (Beachy Head, Longstone, Hartland Point, Anvil Point, Hurst Point, and Eddystone), has proven invaluable in supporting Operation TELIC and ongoing operations in Iraq. These ships are operated by a commercial shipping consortium, AWSR Shipping Ltd. Under the terms of its agreement with the MoD, AWSR typically commits four of the ships to MoD tasking requirements, leaving a further two ro-ro vessels in the commercial market, to be called-out in time of crisis. These are crewed by 180 Sponsored Reserves, provided by AWSR but serving with the RN Reserve. See "Sponsored Reserves."

30. Supporting Operations, Met Office Website, available from *www.metoffice.gov.uk/defence/mmu,* accessed May 20, 2014.

31. A green paper is a tentative government report and consultation document of policy proposals for debate and discussion,

without any commitment to action; the first step in changing the law. Green papers may result in the production of a white paper.

32. The Independent Commission to Review the United Kingdom's Reserve Forces, p. 6.

33. A white paper is an authoritative report or guide helping readers understand an issue, solve a problem, or make a decision.

34. *Reserves in the Future Force 2020: Valuable and Valued*, p. 8.

35. The Chief of Defence Personnel, is the Senior Responsible Owner for FR20 and is accountable to the Reserves Executive Committee, chaired by the Vice-Chief of the Defence Staff, and ultimately to the Secretary of State for Defence for the delivery of the future Reserve Forces.

36. *Reserves in the Future Force 2020: Valuable and Valued*, pp. 10-15.

37. Zoe Morrison, Wendy Loretto, and Sarah Cunningham-Burley, *Future Reserves 2020: Understanding the Factors that Affect Support for Reserve Service — a preliminary study prepared for the United Kingdom Ministry of Defence*, Edinburgh, Scotland: University of Edinburgh, Centre for Families and Relationships, March 2013, p. 13.

38. *Ibid.*, p. 3.

39. *Reserves in the Future Force 2020: Valuable and Valued*, p. 31.

40. *Ibid.*, p. 32.

41. Louisa Brooke-Holland, "Future Reserves 2020," SN06733, London, UK: House of Commons, International Affairs and Defence Section, October 3, 2013, p. 4.

42. The Kitemark is a symbol of trust, integrity, and quality recognized worldwide and described as a 'Business Superbrand'. It is a registered certification mark owned and awarded by the British Standards Institution (BSI), originally developed by the BSI. Kitemark website available from *www.kitemark.com/about-kitemark/*, accessed May 18, 2014.

43. *Consultation Launched on the Future of Britain's Reserve Forces*, London, UK: Ministry of Defence, November 8, 2012, available from *https://www.gov.uk/government/news/consultation-launched-on-the-future-of-britains-Reserve-forces*, accessed May 10, 2014.

44. *Reserves in the Future Force 2020: Valuable and Valued*, p. 8.

45. Two weeks leave after the birth is mandatory by law.

46. Statutory Maternity Pay consists of 90 percent of average earnings (before tax) for the first 6 weeks followed by £138.18 or 90 percent of average weekly earnings for the following 33 weeks. See *Maternity Pay and Leave*, UK Government website, available from *https://www.gov.uk/maternity-pay-leave/leave*, accessed May 18, 2014.

47. The entitlement for Paternity pay and leave is available when your partner is having a baby or a child is adopted. This typically consists of between 1 and 2 weeks paid Ordinary Paternity Leave, as well as up to 26 week's Additional Paternity Leave, if the mother/co-adopter returns to work. See UK Government Website, available from *https://www.gov.uk/paternity-pay-leave*, accessed May 18, 2014.

48. Philippa Tucker, Response to Ministry of Defence consultation on "Future Reserves 2020: Delivering the Nation's Security Together," Corby and London, UK: Chartered Management Institute, January 2013, available from *www.managers.org.uk/sites/default/files/Future%20Reserves%202020%20-%20consultation%20response.pdf*, accessed May 8, 2014.

49. *Ibid.*

50. Richard Tyler, "Employers Benefit from Afghan Tours," *Daily Telegraph*, July 13, 2014.

51. *Army 2020*, HC 263, Session 2014-15, London, UK: Ministry of Defence, National Audit Office, June 11, 2014, pp. 7-8.

52. *Ibid.*

53. Professor Connelly is also an officer in the British Army Reserve, currently serving as SO1 G1 Policy and Plans, HQ Support Command.

54. E-mail correspondence with author, July 2014.

55. *Army 2020*, HC 263, Session 2014-15.

56. *Ibid.*

57. *Ibid.*

58. Interviews conducted with UK Army Reservists between April and June 2014.

59. Peter Quentin, *RUSI Journal*, Vol. 33, No 2, March 13, 2014, pp. 5-7, available from *https://www.rusi.org/publications/newsbrief/ref:A514077C33D4E6/#.U2t3_1d7Jps*, accessed May 8, 2014.

60. Harding.

61. As of April 2012. *TSP7 – UK Reserve Forces and Cadets: April 2013*, Defence Statistics (Tri Service) London, UK: Ministry of Defence, November 28, 2013.

62. TSP7.

63. Harding.

64. E-mail correspondence with author, July 2014.

65. Interviews conducted with serving members of the Reserve Forces in the Army Reserve conducted between March 2014 and May 2014.

66. Interviews conducted with members of 256 Field Hospital, May 1, 2014.

67. Harding.

68. *Ibid.*

69. Winnie Agbonlahor, "'Playing with Fire," *Civil Service World*, October 14, 2013, available from *www.civilserviceworld.com/playing-with-fire-2*, accessed April 28, 2014.

70. Caroline Wyatt, "Has Britain's Defence Budget Been Cut Too Much?" *BBC News,* February 24, 2014, available from *www.bbc.co.uk/news/uk-26271018*, accessed May 13, 2014.

71. Colonel Ted Spain U.S. Army (Ret.) and Terry Turchie, Deputy Assistant Director, Federal Bureau of Investigation, *Breaking Iraq: The Ten Mistakes That Broke Iraq*, New York: History Publishing Company, 2013.

72. Sydney J. Freedberg, Jr., "National Guard Commanders Rise in Revolt Amongst Active Army; MG Rossi Questions Guard Combat Role" *Breaking Defence*, March 11, 2014, available from *breakingdefense.com/2014/03/national-guard-commanders-rise-in-revolt-against-active-army-mg-ross-questions-guard-combat-role/*, accessed April 29, 2014.

73. Dr. Patrick Allen, PMP, Johns Hopkins University, retired as a full colonel in the U.S. Army Reserves in 2002. He has 21 years of service, 4 of which were active service, with the remainder in the U.S. Army Reserves involved with correspondence and 2-week tours at various locations around the United States and in Germany.

74. Interview with Dr. Patrick Allen, April 13, 2014.

75. Vince Connelly, "Cultural Differences between the Regular Army and the TA as Barriers to Integration," Unpublished paper prepared for UK Ministry of Defense, Directorate of Personnel Capability, January 2013, p. 11.

76. Penny Dick and Rosie Hyde, *Consent as Resistance, Resistance as Consent: Re-Reading Part-Time Professionals' Acceptance of Their Marginal Positions, Gender, Work & Organization*, Vol. 13, Issue 6, November 2006, pp. 543–564.

77. Shima D. Keene, "Bullfinch Review: The Use of Financial and Criminal Intelligence in the context of tackling Child Sexual Exploitation" Unpublished report (restricted) produced for Thames Valley Police, UK, March 2014.

78. Connelly, "Cultural Differences between the Regular Army and the TA as Barriers to Integration," p. 19.

79. The Royal United Services Institute (RUSI) is an independent think tank engaged in defense and security research, founded in 1831 by the Duke of Wellington.

80. Peter Quentin, *RUSI Journal*, Vol. 33, No. 2, March 13, pp. 5-7, available from *https://www.rusi.org/publications/newsbrief/ref:A514077C33D4E6/#.U2t3_1d7Jps*, accessed May 8, 2014.

81. "Become a Reservist," Lafayette Hill, PA: NHS Services, available from *www.nhscareers.nhs.uk/working-in-the-nhs/developing-your-career/become-a-Reservist/*, accessed May 16, 2014.

82. Interviews held with Medical Corps staff from 256 Field Hospital, London, UK. See Appendix A for further details.

83. The most common mistake is to consider "intelligence" as synonymous with "information." Information is not intelligence. Information plus analysis equals intelligence. So without analysis, there is no intelligence. In other words, Intelligence is not what is collected; it is what is produced after collected data is evaluated and analyzed. As such, analysis requires thoughtful contemplation that results in conclusions and recommendations. Computers may assist with analysis by compiling large amounts of data into an easily accessible format, but this is still only collated data; it is not analyzed data or information, and it falls far short of being intelligence.

84. The Review of Intelligence on Weapons of Mass Destruction, widely known as the Butler Review after its chairman Lord Robin Butler of Brockwell, published by the British government on July 4, 2004. The Review examined the intelligence on Iraq's weapons of mass destruction which played a key part in the Government's decision to invade Iraq (as part of the U.S.-led coalition) in 2003.

85. Lord Robin Butler *et al.*, "Review of Intelligence on Weapons of Mass Destruction," London, UK: House of Commons Publication, July 14, 2004.

86. *Ibid.*

87. "Securing Britain in an Age of Uncertainty," *The Strategic Defence and Security Review*, HM Government Cm 7948, October 2010.

88. "Exercise Agile Warrior and Future Development of UK Land Forces," RUSI Occasional Paper, London, UK, May 2011.

89. *Strategic Trends Program, Future Character of Conflict*, London, UK: Ministry of Defence, Developments, Concepts and Doctrine Centre, February 2, 2010.

90. *Allied Administrative Publication (AAP)-6: NATO Glossary of Terms and Definitions*, Brussels, Belgium, August 7, 2000, available from *https://wss.apan.org/432/Files/Events/TE-03/Supporting%20Documents/NATO%20Terms%20%20and%20 Definitions.pdf*, accessed May 15, 2014.

91. This conceptual framework consists of four environments: cultural, institutional (including political and military), technological, and physical.

92. *Joint Doctrine Publication 04: Understanding*, London, UK: Ministry of Defence, Developments, Concepts and Doctrine Centre, December 2010.

93. Pashto (alternatively spelled Pukhto, Pakhto or Pushto), also known historically as Afghani and Pathani, is the native language of the Pashtun people of South-Central Asia. Pashto is one of the two official languages of Afghanistan (the other being Dari [Farsi]), and is also spoken as a regional language in western and northwestern Pakistan and among the Pashtun diaspora around the world.

94. Wanetsi, or Waneci, is a Pashto dialect which is spoken by a small population of Tareen tribes in Pakistan and Afghanistan, primarily in Harnai and Sinjawi area east of Quetta, northern Balochistan, Pakistan.

95. Ben Farmer, "Army Struggling to Find Recruits since System Was Overhauled to Cut Costs," Defence Correspondent,

The Telegraph (London), October 7, 2013, available from *www. telegraph.co.uk/news/uknews/defence/10359743/Army-struggling-to-find-recruits-since-system-was-overhauled-to-cut-costs.html*, accessed May 20, 2014.

96. *Ibid.*

97. *Ibid.*

98. Interview with serving Warrant Officer, 256 Field Hospital, May 1, 2014.

99. Interviews conducted with members of the Reserve forces carried out between January and July 2014.

100. 36th Air Refueling Squadron (336 ARS) is a United States Air Force Reserve squadron assigned to the 452d Operations Group stationed at March Joint Air Reserve Base, CA. The squadron is a corollary unit of the active duty 92d Air Refueling Squadron, 92d Air Refueling Wing (92 ARW), Fairchild Air Force Base, WA.

101. "US Army Human Resource Command (HRC) Enlisted EMF History Chart," available from *https:// pamxxi.armyg1. army.mil/Select/SelectMosUnclas.aspx.*

U.S. ARMY WAR COLLEGE

Major General William E. Rapp
Commandant

*****

STRATEGIC STUDIES INSTITUTE
and
U.S. ARMY WAR COLLEGE PRESS

Director
Professor Douglas C. Lovelace, Jr.

Director of Research
Dr. Steven K. Metz

Author
Dr. Shima D. Keene

Editor for Production
Dr. James G. Pierce

Publications Assistant
Ms. Rita A. Rummel

*****

Composition
Mrs. Jennifer E. Nevil